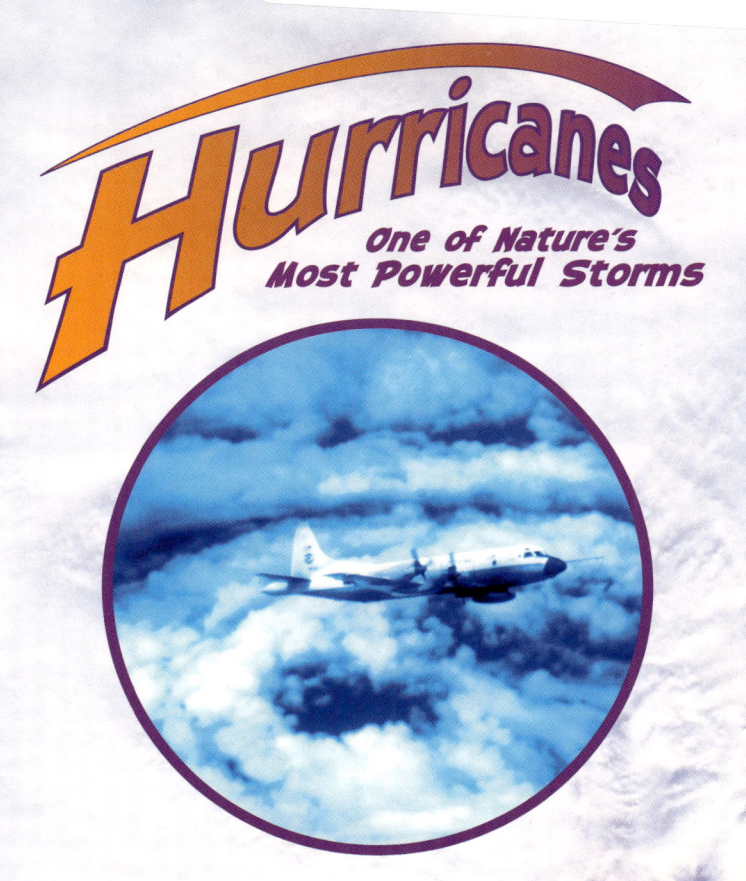

Hurricanes
One of Nature's Most Powerful Storms

By Charles Higgins
and Regina Higgins

CELEBRATION PRESS
Pearson Learning Group

Contents

How Hurricanes Form 3

A Hurricane's Fury 9

Hurricanes by the Numbers . . .15

Storm Surges and Flash Floods .21

Hurricane Safety 27

Glossary 32

Index . . . . .Inside Back Cover

How Hurricanes Form

The wind comes sweeping in gently at first, making the trees bend and sway. The white-capped waves slowly grow rougher, until their spray reaches as high as the docks. The pounding rain suddenly begins to pour down.

Then the fury of the storm hits full blast. Telephone poles and trees snap under its power. The roofs of some houses rattle, then lift, and are carried away by the wind. The wind-whipped sea rises 10 feet and pounds the shore. The crashing waves flood every house and street for a mile inland. What kind of storm could possibly create such destruction?

Hurricanes are violent storms that occur in the North Atlantic Ocean. They have winds of more than 74 miles per hour (mph). They begin over warm ocean water. Then, if conditions are right, they move quickly and grow stronger. When a hurricane reaches land, the storm can bring destructive winds and heavy rain.

From a weather **satellite**, a hurricane looks like a flat doughnut. Like a doughnut, the hurricane has a hole in the middle called the **eye**. This is the storm's calm center. In some large hurricanes, the eye can be more than 40 miles wide.

A ring of tall, dark clouds, called the **eyewall**, circles the eye of the hurricane. The hurricane's strongest winds occur in the eyewall. The winds can blow as fast as 200 mph.

A storm at sea forms as warm water evaporates and rises, creating an area of low pressure. The air around this low pressure rushes in to take the place of the rising air.

HURRICANE STRUCTURE

- Eye
- Eyewall
- Spiral rain bands
- Counterclockwise rotation

This creates more moist air that rises and cools. When the cooling air **condenses**, rain clouds form. Weather scientists, or meteorologists, call this a **tropical disturbance**.

Usually the rain in a tropical disturbance falls within a few hours after the clouds form. Then the clouds begin to break up. Sometimes, however, the clouds continue to build. They gather strength from the large amount of warm, moist air rising and cooling. This energy also helps to form winds. Now, the system becomes a **tropical depression**.

Because of the rotation of Earth, the winds drawn into this low-pressure system move in a curving path. Scientists call this tendency for winds to spiral the **Coriolis effect**. North of the equator, winds circle counterclockwise. South of the equator, winds circle clockwise. These circling winds are the reason we call these storms "cyclones."

The spiraling winds cause the pressure to drop quickly at the storm's center. The low pressure draws in even more warm, moist air. This causes the winds to grow stronger and faster. If the winds blow faster than 38 mph, meteorologists call it a **tropical storm**.

Meteorologists track every tropical storm carefully. They use satellites and information from ships in the area. If the wind speed of a tropical storm in the North Atlantic reaches greater than 74 mph, it officially becomes a hurricane.

HURRICANE PATHS

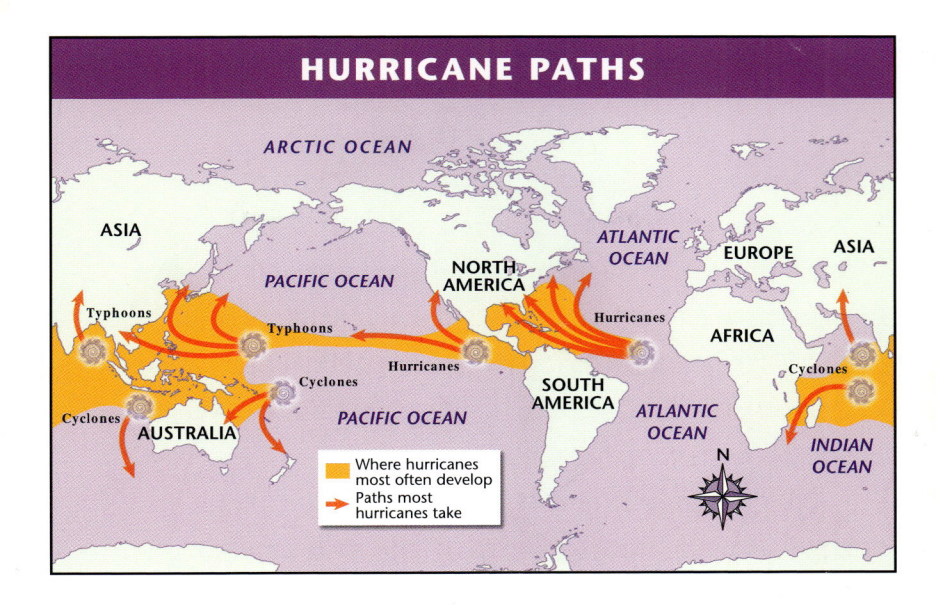

Meteorologists give every tropical storm and hurricane its own name. Names of storms that have caused a huge amount of damage are never used again.

Since 1953, the World Meteorological Organization has created lists of names for tropical storms. These lists are in alphabetical order. For example, the first tropical storm of the year might be named Antonio, the second Beatrice, the third Charles, and so on. Since few names begin with q, u, x, y, and z, these letters are not used.

Hurricanes in the North Atlantic Ocean usually occur from June through November. Every hurricane begins as a low-pressure system. However, not every low-pressure system becomes a hurricane. In order for a hurricane to develop, some special water and wind conditions must occur. Otherwise, the storm will fall apart.

Most hurricanes that hit the Caribbean and the United States begin in the warm waters off the west coast of Africa. When the storm grows in strength, it starts to move westward across the Atlantic Ocean. The warm ocean water feeds the storm. By the time it reaches the Caribbean, winds may reach speeds greater than 150 mph.

A typical hurricane in the North Atlantic follows a pattern as it develops. However, it can twist and turn in unexpected directions. When it does, meteorologists wonder whether the hurricane will make **landfall** or turn back out to sea. They also wonder where it will hit and with what strength.

A Hurricane's Fury

On September 16, 1999, a small plane filled with weather equipment flew through the clouds. A team of weather scientists from the Hurricane Research Division was headed for the worst.

Hurricane Floyd was charging up the East Coast of the United States. To determine where and when Floyd might turn next, the scientists had to take readings at several locations. That meant flying directly into the hurricane itself.

Weather scientists brave a raging hurricane to take readings from inside an NOAA P3.

The clouds grew grayer and wetter. The plane began to sway and bump like a car on a rocky road. The scientists took their first wind-speed reading. The wind was only 65 mph—not even hurricane speed. As they approached the eyewall, they knew the readings would get higher.

The passengers braced themselves as the plane slammed into the eyewall. The wind's speed readings jumped. The scientists recorded the figures.

Caught in the hurricane's whirling force, the pilot made his way toward the eye. At the calm center of the storm, the sky was blue and the wind was low. However, the peace was only temporary. The plane was headed for the opposite eyewall to take more readings.

After the wild ride through Floyd, the team flew over Wilmington, North Carolina. The coastal city was deserted and already beginning to flood. Almost 2 million people left their homes looking for safety.

Meteorologists had spotted Floyd as a tropical wave on September 2, 1999. On September 7, it was considered a tropical depression. By the next day, the system had moved quickly northwest and developed into a tropical storm. Tropical storm Floyd became a hurricane on September 10.

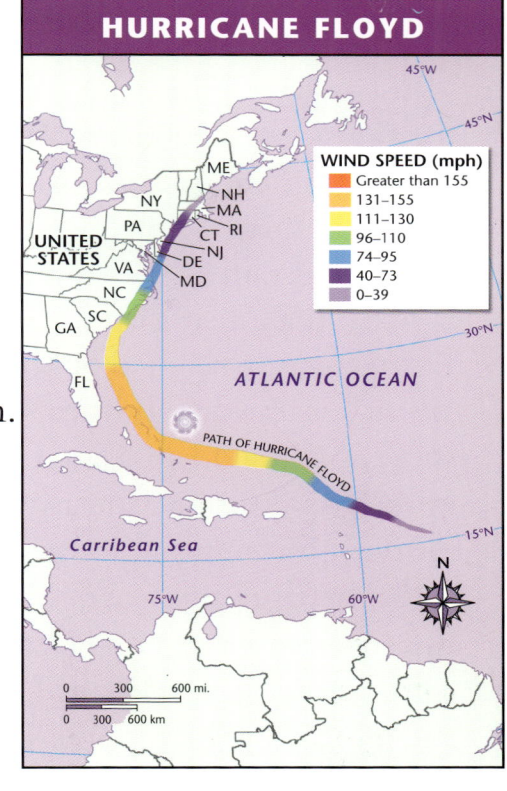

HURRICANE FLOYD

WIND SPEED (mph)
- Greater than 155
- 131–155
- 111–130
- 96–110
- 74–95
- 40–73
- 0–39

PATH OF HURRICANE FLOYD

Meteorologists tracked Floyd across the Atlantic to the Caribbean. Would Floyd turn west and hit the coast of Florida? Would it continue up the eastern seaboard? They weren't sure what Floyd was going to do.

Just in case, Floridians prepared themselves for the storm. Quickly, they boarded up their houses and **evacuated** coastal cities. Floyd, however, turned northward, bringing its high winds and rain to North Carolina.

At landfall near Cape Fear, North Carolina, Floyd's winds reached about 104 mph. Its storm surge reached from 9 to 10 feet. Storm surge is the sudden rising of the water on the coast. Floyd dropped just over 19 inches of rain on Wilmington, North Carolina.

By the time the storm had passed through the state, rain and winds had destroyed more than 7,000 homes. Farms looked like lakes. More than 45,000 people had to go to shelters because their homes had been destroyed. Hurricane Floyd became the worst natural disaster in the history of North Carolina.

Once it left North Carolina, Hurricane Floyd pounded the eastern seaboard for several days with wind and rain.

The storm continued as far north as Canada. Even nearing the end of its rampage up the coast, Floyd had enough power to soak Brewster, New York, with 13.7 inches of rain.

By September 17, Floyd's fury was coming to an end. Its northward path was taking it farther and farther from warm waters. As a result, the hurricane began to lose power. By the time Floyd reached Canada, it had lost power. When it moved east, the storm became just another low-pressure system in the Atlantic Ocean.

Floyd's rains flooded North Carolina, causing the state's worst natural disaster.

Flood waters from Hurricane Floyd left this parking lot under water.

    Floyd caused about $6 billion in property damage. The storm also proved to be the deadliest hurricane in the United States since Hurricane Agnes in 1972. Floyd killed 57 people in its path. Most of those who were killed drowned in the severe flooding that the hurricane's rains had created inland. Millions of animals were also drowned, and huge numbers of fish were killed by pollution washed into waterways.

Hurricanes by the Numbers

Every year when the hurricane season begins, weather forecasters report on the number of hurricanes we may expect. How are these predictions made?

Max Mayfield is one of the people who predicts how many hurricanes there will be. He works with other meteorologists at the National Hurricane Center. They look at changes in ocean temperature and in wind patterns. They also look at historical data. They use this data to find clues about approaching hurricanes.

National Hurricane Center Director Max Mayfield studies satellite images of a hurricane.

Modern hurricane forecasting began with Father Benito Vi-es. Father Vi-es was a Catholic priest who lived in Cuba more than 100 years ago. He closely observed the weather many times a day. After a hurricane, he looked through the debris and questioned people who had survived.

On September 11, 1875, Vi-es asked a local newspaper to make a special announcement. He believed that a hurricane was heading for the southern coast of the island. He thought that it would arrive in about two days.

Vi-es's prediction was right. His announcement apparently was the first hurricane warning in the Americas. It saved many lives. Vi-es died on July 23, 1893. His students continued his work.

Today, forecasters use many of the same methods Vi-es did. Modern forecasters, however, have much better tools. **Radar** is one of these tools. With radar, scientists can observe weather systems hundreds of miles away.

Doppler radar of Hurricane Floyd as it pounds the Bahamas

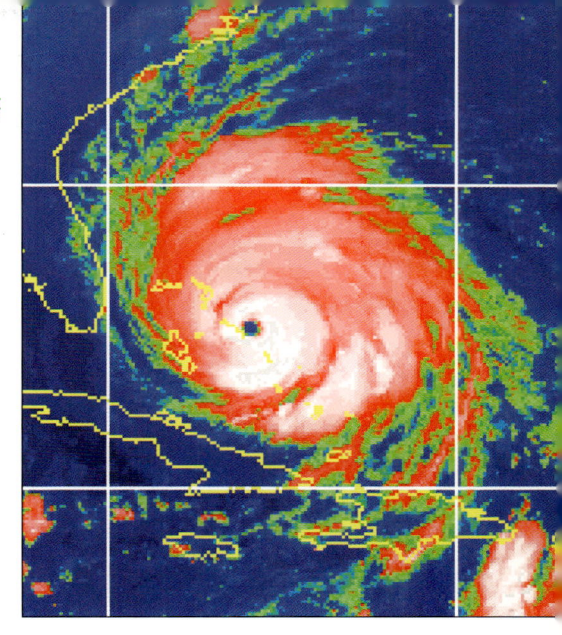

Radar was first used in World War II to locate ships and planes. Now, radar helps meteorologists keep track of storms. **Doppler radar** measures wind speed and direction. This information can provide clues about how fast a storm is moving and where it might be headed.

Weather balloons can also provide information about developing hurricanes. Researchers release these balloons. The balloons take readings of temperature, air pressure, and wind speed from high in the atmosphere.

Another way to gather information is to drop equipment into the sea from airplanes. Scientists onboard the plane send the data back to computers at the National Hurricane Center.

Since 1960, meteorologists have used satellites to observe storm systems. In photos taken by satellites, scientists can view the gathering clouds that may become hurricanes.

Weather computers receive the information sent from satellites, weather planes, and balloons. Scientists use the data to make predictions and to give warnings. Computers can also create models of developing storms. Scientists can work with these models to judge how serious a storm will be.

The National Weather Service may use radar readings and other data to announce a hurricane watch or warning. A watch means that a hurricane may hit an area within 36 hours. A warning means that a hurricane is expected within 24 hours. Local officials may order an evacuation.

Saffir-Simpson Hurricane Scale

Category	Winds	Damage
1	74–95 mph	damage to trees and shrubs; storm surge 4–5 feet
2	96–110 mph	damage to roofs, doors, and windows; some flooding; storm surge 6–8 feet
3	111–130 mph	large trees down; structural damage to small houses and mobile homes; coastal evacuation due to flooding; storm surge 9–12 feet
4	131–155 mph	roofs of small houses collapse; flooding; evacuation of people as far as 6 miles inland; storm surge 13–18 feet
5	greater than 155 mph	catastrophic; some buildings collapse entirely, doors damaged on others; mass evacuation of everyone within 10 miles of the coast; storm surge higher than 18 feet

Scientists use satellite photos, wind readings, and computer models to tell how strong a hurricane is. Then scientists judge how much damage a storm may cause using the **Saffir-Simpson Hurricane Scale**.

The Saffir-Simpson Hurricane Scale ranges from Category 1 to Category 5. A Category 1 hurricane may seem no worse than a bad rainstorm. A Category 5 hurricane will bring great destruction. A Category 2 or 3 hurricane can create as much damage as a Category 5 if it stays in one area for too long.

In 1998, Hurricane Georges was a low category hurricane that caused a lot damage. It had a steady supply of warm water to feed its winds. As a result, it gained a wind speed of 150 mph. The hurricane lasted for more than a week in the Caribbean near the southern United States.

By the time the hurricane hit the Florida Keys, its winds had slowed to 90 mph. It became a Category 1 storm. However, it still caused a lot of damage. Over its long life, Georges brought as much destruction as it would have if it had been a much stronger hurricane. It destroyed tens of thousands of homes throughout the Caribbean islands. In the Dominican Republic, 90 percent of banana and other plantations were destroyed. In Florida, the hurricane dumped 20 to 30 inches of rain, causing damaging floods. More than 150 people had to be rescued from their homes. In total, Hurricane Georges killed more than 600 people.

Storm Surges and Flash Floods

In August 1969, Hurricane Camille moved across the Gulf of Mexico. It was heading toward Mississippi. Computers at the National Hurricane Center created models. A new computer program made a surprising prediction about the storm surge. It said it could reach higher than 20 feet.

At that time, meteorologists never mentioned exact wind speeds and surge figures. A hurricane report would simply warn of "strong winds" or "high water."

Meteorologist Robert Simpson believed that the storm surge was going to be dangerous. Local officials began evacuating people.

The water rose to 22.6 feet in Pass Christian, Mississippi. The storm surge along the Gulf Coast killed 172 people. If Simpson had not given the warning, many more people might have died.

A stranded horse stands on top of the rubble from houses destroyed by the Galveston hurricane in Galveston, Texas, in 1900.

Most people think that a hurricane's high winds cause most of the damage. It's true that high winds are dangerous. In 1992, Hurricane Andrew's 145 to 150 mph winds hit the coast of southern Florida in the middle of the night. By dawn, more than 25,000 homes had been destroyed.

However, the high water from a storm surge is even more deadly. In 1900, a hurricane hit Galveston, Texas. High water from the storm surge killed about 6,000 people.

The storm surge of a hurricane begins in the eye. The low pressure in the eye pulls up water from the sea. Then it holds the water like liquid in a straw when someone holds a finger over one end of the straw. The storm's winds push the water ahead of the eye.

When the storm hits the shore, this huge amount of water suddenly raises the sea level up to 15 feet or more. Tons of water may rush onto the coast. Wild waves crash on the shore, smashing everything in their path.

Hurricane Floyd whirls off the coast of South Carolina.

Sometimes, the geography of an area can make a storm surge even more forceful. The Bay of Bengal is located on the eastern side of the Indian Ocean. The bay narrows in the north. Like liquid flowing through a funnel, water from a storm surge rushes onto land.

In 1970, a tropical cyclone hit this area. The area was then called East Pakistan. About 266,000 people drowned.

East Pakistanis looked for help from their government. They were angry over the small amount of aid they received. They changed their government and formed their own country called Bangladesh.

Tropical cyclones still hit the Bay of Bengal. However, warning systems have been improved. Now, there is more time for people to evacuate.

There are also concrete shelters along the coast. They were built high enough to keep people safe from the storm surge. As a result, there are fewer deaths from tropical cyclones in Bangladesh.

Famous American Hurricanes

Hurricane Name	Year	Places Affected
Galveston	1900	Galveston, Texas
Hazel	1954	Caribbean; eastern U.S.
Donna	1960	Caribbean; eastern U.S.
Camille	1969	Gulf Coast; mid-Atlantic states
Agnes	1972	Mexio; southern and northeastern U.S.
Hugo	1989	Caribbean; southeastern U.S.
Andrew	1992	Florida; Gulf Coast; southeastern U.S.
Georges	1998	Caribbean; Florida
Floyd	1999	eastern U.S.

Improved warning systems have also helped reduce deaths from storm surges in the United States. Most people living along a coast are prepared to evacuate during a warning.

High water from hurricanes can also be dangerous to people living inland. Storm surges pour water into rivers. These rivers may overflow and cause floods.

As the hurricane drops rain, the rain fills rivers and streams inland. A large amount of rainfall over a few hours or days can cause serious flooding.

Many people living 100 or more miles from the shore believe they are safe from hurricanes. However, they can be wrong. The greatest danger to inland communities comes from flooding. Fifty of the 57 people who died during Hurricane Floyd in 1999 drowned in floods from rivers.

During Hurricane Floyd, the Tar River in North Carolina rose 24 feet above flood level. The river overflowed in all directions. It flooded across miles of low-lying land. As Floyd moved up the East Coast, it continued to bring flooding. In Bound Brook, New Jersey, the Raritan River rose over its banks and flooded much of the town.

Flooding often takes people by surprise. In a few hours, rain from a hurricane can make even a small river or stream overflow. This unexpected flooding can be deadly. Keeping people informed of the dangers of flooding will be the next important challenge for forecasters.

Hurricane Safety

Suppose the National Weather Service warns that a hurricane is on the way. What should people do? Information and preparation are the two most important safety tools during a hurricane.

At the beginning of hurricane season, coastal families should check their storm shutters. Strong shutters may keep houses safe from damaging winds. People must also make sure they have a working battery-operated radio, a flashlight, food and water, and first-aid supplies.

People should also make a family plan. A family plan is important when evacuation becomes necessary. Some coastal families plan to stay with friends or families. Others will go to motels or shelters.

People who evacuate should take care of their pets. Pets who cannot evacuate with their owners can go to pet shelters.

When a hurricane strikes, officials also need to be ready. During Hurricane Floyd, many people evacuated the port city of Charleston. They headed inland on Interstate 26. To speed up this traffic, the governor of South Carolina gave a special order. He made a section of the highway a one-way road leading away from the path of the hurricane.

There are things people should do when a hurricane watch is announced. They should check their supplies, fill their cars with gasoline, and prepare their houses.

In an emergency, people can evacuate by car along designated highways.

People should also listen for special news bulletins. News bulletins may announce that the storm has moved out of the area. They may also say that the storm watch has become a warning.

If officials order an evacuation, people should leave quickly. Anyone who stays home during a hurricane should stay away from windows. The high winds can shatter glass and cause serious injury.

The eye of the storm is calm. Once the eye passes, hurricane winds will start up again without warning. Because they form part of the eyewall, these winds will be the worst of the storm.

High water creates the greatest danger in a hurricane. Therefore, people should move to high ground whether they are on the coast or inland. They should also pay special attention to news about flooding. In a hurricane, even a small stream can suddenly overflow and become dangerous.

Sometimes during an evacuation, owners have to leave their pets behind. It is very difficult for them to leave without taking their pets with them. However, owners are hopeful that they will see their pets again soon.

People should wait for the "all clear" signal from officials. Then they can return to their homes and begin looking for their pets. The first thing people need to do when they look for lost pets is to go to different animal shelters.

In a hurricane, pets need special care and attention.

Once home, people should avoid areas with hurricane damage. Driving in flooded areas can be dangerous. Traffic may get in the way of emergency crews cleaning streets and fixing downed power lines. It may also get in the way of rescue workers trying to help people and animals.

Even after the hurricane is over, people should keep listening for official news. There will be announcements about where and when to get food and clean water. If the hurricane has caused great damage, the government may offer help to rebuild.

Hurricanes will always be a concern in certain areas of the world. They are a natural part of our planet's weather. Fortunately, we live in a time when information about hurricanes can save thousands of lives each year. Today, scientists have the equipment they need to track hurricanes. With the right information and preparation, people have a better chance than ever before of surviving nature's greatest storms.

Glossary

condenses — changes from a gas to a liquid
Coriolis effect — the tendency for winds to begin moving in a circular pattern
Doppler radar — a radar system for detecting direction and speed
evacuated — orderly removal of people from areas during an emergency
eye — the calm center of a hurricane
eyewall — the ring-shaped area of tall clouds surrounding the hurricane's eye, which contains the strongest winds
landfall — the place where a hurricane moves from the sea onto land
radar — a system using radio waves to locate objects
Saffir-Simpson Hurricane Scale — a scale used to measure a hurricane's strength
satellite — an object that is sent into space to gather information
tropical depression — a low-pressure system formed near the equator that is surrounded by winds blowing 38 mph or less
tropical disturbance — a system of low pressure near the equator with growing clouds and showers
tropical storm — a low-pressure system formed near the equator, having inwardly spiraling winds blowing from 39 to 74 mph